My Mind Is

Totally

Mine

BY THE SAME AUTHOR

Won't Tell, Part 1, Part 2, Part 3
(Heart-warming Holiday trilogy)

True Colors
(Memoir)

Gutsy Little Eddie
(A short story)

Formatting Your Fantastic Book
(2018 CIPA EVVY Book Award)

Bully Jake and Grace's Fate
Hats Off to Mr. Boar
(First and second books of this rhyming parody)

Only a Shoebox to His Name
(Memoir)

All paperback and e-books by this author can be found on Amazon.

My Mind Is

Totally

Mine

MARY KORTE
Matt Hinrichs, Illustrator

HAVET PRESS
www.HavetPress.com
Kirkland, Washington

My Mind Is Totally Mine

A sequel to *Bully Jake and Grace's Fate* and *Hats Off to Mr. Boar*, Copyright © 2018 (and revised 2024) by Mary Korte. All rights reserved. No part of this book may be used or reproduced without the author's permission except for brief quotations embodied in reviews. Word meanings in the Glossary are limited to story content. Character names are fictitious.

Grammarly Readability Score: 82.88 (desirable: 60-70)

Grammarly Quality of Writing Score: 99 out of 100.

Cover design and illustrations © 2018 Matt Hinrichs

Havet Press
   www.HavetPress.com

Library of Congress Control Number:
   2017918994

ISBN-978-0-9983132-1-4

Printed in the United States of America

Table of Contents

PART I

Letter to Stepchildren.........1

PART II

My Mind Is Totally Mine .. 21

Glossary 197

My Mind Is Totally Mine

(the third book in a three-part series)

meets the

publishing requirement

for

visually challenged readers.

PART I

Letter to Step-children

Step-children, please know that *most* stepparents are

accepting, loving,

and worthy of your love.

YES,

sometimes stepparents

think they can fix

your emotional pain,

BUT

when they attempt

this impossible task,

they will likely feel

they are going insane.

THAT IS,

until they learn

that fixing your pain

is impossible for them to do;

because even though they try,

they cannot replace

the bio-parent connection in you.

THUS,

as they take on the challenge

of caring for you,

they will find it is best
to put that dream to rest.

IT IS SAD TO SAY,

when you are having

a hurt-filled day,

you might push them away.

BUT MOST STEPPARENTS,

no matter what you do or say,

will not shun you.

OF COURSE,

stepparents will do things that

will make you mad,

BUT

they will also comfort you
when you are feeling sad.

NOT SURPRISINGLY,

after you do something unacceptable,
they will offer you a hug.

AND

if/when they do, hopefully,
you will return

a treasured snug.

Some stepparents—but not all—
will order you around.

THEY OFTEN SAY,

"Go make your bed."

"Put that thing down."

"Brush your teeth."

"HEY.

Dishes go in the sink."

"Take out the trash."

"WHAT?

You colored your hair pink?"

"YES, I DID. SO, WHAT!"

"Well, that was rash.

And I suppose,
since you're looking sassy fine,
you're going out tonight?"

"YEAH."

"School tomorrow, so be home by nine.
And don't be late."

NOW, IF IT HAPPENS

to be your fate

to have a stepparent
who says these things—
plus, a whole lot more—
I suggest you thank your lucky stars,
because a caring stepparent

you surely did score.

Some days, when you are in a hurry,
stepparents will gladly spread
whatever you want
upon your sandwich bread.
And often,
after a hectic push-pull day,

they will willingly

give you a kiss goodnight
and tuck you snugly into bed.

AS CHAUFFEURS,

stepparents will transport you

to doctors, dentists

and all sorts of lessons,

pLUS,

they will drop you off

and pick you up

from your cross-country run,

football, baseball, basketball,

soccer and tennis,

OR

whatever else you do for fun.

ALSO

stepparents will be supportive

by attending *your* school play.

And, yes, they will

embarrass you

by speaking up
at your school's monthly PTA.

FOR SURE,

if you are a girl,

they will teach you

to primp with care;
if you are a boy,
they will understand
if you take on a dare.

oOPs...

That was NOT fair.

Girls take on dares, too.

Oh, and from stepparents,
you can expect firmness and
kindness, plus

love that never ends;

AND

that includes permission to

having sleepovers

with your chummy friends.

OF COURSE,

stepparents will lay down the law—

the why-of-which

you may not understand—

BUT DISCIPLINE

comes with the mix

of making sure you have

the best childhood ever

before your feet

onto adult ground

get <u>transfixed</u>.

AND ALWAYS,

stepparents hope and pray

that their efforts

will pay off someday.

NO, NO, NO!

Not only someday,

BUT

all along the way.

YES,

you can expect stepparents

to do caring things,

BUT

did you know,
they will also put up with
your misbehaving flings?

AND . . .

before you know it,

time will pass.

AH, YES, MR. LAD AND MISS LASS,

you will grow up,

AND

when that happens,

they will

look you in the eye

and say,

"Thanks for letting me

be there by your side.

And even though at times

it was a bumpy ride,

we made it through.

And I must say,

'I am very proud of you.'"

THEN,

as you both emit heartfelt sighs,

tears will likely cloud your eyes.

YOUNG READERS,

as you read on in this book,

please know,

mentally challenged stepparents
who abuse their stepchildren—
which, of course,
no way is cool—

are the exception,

NOT THE RULE.

PART II

PART 1

My Mind Is Totally Mine

Back in 1953,

shortly after

Mr. Boar's fifth graders defeated

Mr. Cock Rooster's

sixth graders

in an unplanned spelling bee,

Miss Maggie McPhee,

a twelve-year-old

in Mr. Cock-Rooster's class,
labeled by many as

poor white trash . . .

WELL,

Mr. Boar's point of view,

I.E.,

If you don't

get a good education,

poverty might become

your life-long vocation,

prompts Miss Maggie McPhee

to construe

what she needs to do

SO THAT

when she grows up,

without a doubt,

no one

will go about

referring to her as

poor white trash.

TO RECAP...

back in 1953,
sometime during
the first week of May,
Mr. Cock-Rooster, upon awakening

$oozy$ and $dizzy$,

decides to take leave for the day.

BEING

both the principal and teacher at
Pine Township Elementary School
near Michigan City, Indiana,
in the countryside of *America[na]*,

HE,

to his

sixth-grade students,

is viewed as:

"WOW!

Are you ever cool."

And why is this so?

WELL, SIMPLY PUT,

it is because with his students,

never does he *ever*

enforce any rule.

ON THE OTHER HAND,

the fifth-grade teacher, Mr. Boar—

tolerating no rowdiness

or discontent—

expects his students

to toe the line,

to keep their noses to the grind.

THUS,

in learning,

they are doing just fine.

WELL, MR. BOAR,

by no means a fool,

at no time asks Mr. Cock-Rooster
why he chose a teaching career.

FOR YOU SEE,

despite knowing the
principal/teacher's twenty-nine
FAIRLY FINE cocky chicks
have learned *nothing* all year,
he strongly believes

it is NOT his place

to interfere.

BUT, OH,

on that day in early May,
the hullabaloo in room 104,
Mr. Boar could hardly endure.

BOOM, BANG, THUMP, CLUNK

WHAT?

Another kid-antics collision?

with fists clenched,

and brow sweat-drenched,
Mr. Boar,
besieged with indecision,
mutters,

"Should I, or

should I not

take on this mission?

OH, AND

GALLOPING HOOPSTER,

since Mr. Cock-Rooster

is absent today,

dare I take charge

of his <u>tumultuous</u> lot,

to whom he has NOT

[all year]

one lesson taught?

CRIMINY,

Since the start of this school day,

those cocky chicks have done nothing

but play, play, play.

AND

if I don't stop their senseless <u>felicity</u>,

might I be

$_g$u^{i}l^{t}y ^{o}f c$_o$$\underline{m}$$\underline{p}$licity?

OR,

WORSE YET,

if I interfere,

will I gain naught

but a blight

on my teaching career?

RAZZLE-DAZZLE STINGRAY . . .

Where's that substitute teacher?

What's causing her delay?

I KNOW

The bell rang over an hour ago,

AND

$_t$r^{a}ff^{i}c by n^{o}w

should not be that slow."

Frustrated and frazzled
by the cocky chicks'
constant tempest squall,
Mr. Boar decides,

to no longer stall.

SMOOTHLY,

LIKE A LOONEY-TUNE SNAFU,

he, mirroring a slothful shrew —
and to his conscience staying true —

strut, strut, struts

straight down the hall.

OH, MY . . .

advancing like a spy

in an old movie clip,
slowly, soundlessly, he doth slip
through Mr. Cock-Rooster's
classroom door.

BEYOND THERE,

simulating a Pink Panther dare,
he stands with

his eyes in a stare,

choking back his dismay
as he takes in the disarray.

of Mr. Cock-Rooster's twenty-nine
OUT-OF-LINE <u>renegades</u>

HOP-HOP-HOPPING

from

chair-to-chair;

AND OF

airplanes and spitballs

flying through the air;

AND OF

bubblegum bubbles

going

POPPITY-POP-POP-POP;

AND OF

yelling and screaming

that needs to STOP!

TETHERED TIPSY TICKS . . .

As he stares at the twenty-nine

OUT-OF-LINE cocky chicks —

one, for sure,

a tyrannical bully —

all engaged in poppycock foolery,

he mumbles, "So, this is what's

been going on in here

this whole school year!"

As jeers and sneers

fall upon his ears,

Mr. Boar thinks,

Oh, how unfortunate.

All twenty-nine

of these FAIRLY FINE—

but out of line—

cocky chicks I cannot dismiss,

FOR

in their studies

for eight months straight

they have been remiss.

SADLY,

unlike kids

in tai chi training,

their brains are waning

six hundred stories below

stupidity's abyss.

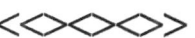

JERK-WATER TIDE . . .

One by one,

the renegades spot Mr. Boar

standing just inside

their classroom door.

AND

as they do,

down, down, down

comes

the volume of

their theatrical uproar.

INSTANTLY,

voices drop

to a chickadee squeak

as each one whispers

this fright-induced tweet:

"Oh, no!

It's Mr. Boar."

Seconds after all twenty-nine
NOT-SO-FINE cocky chicks—
all longing to be somewhere

other than there—

quiver under Mr. Boar's stare,
they each scramble
for *his* or *her* chair.

AND STRAIGHTAWAY,

all eyes orient toward Mr. Boar,

as he, wasting no time,

rattles off

the many conniving jollies

of their

year-long follies.

AND BLASTED BALDERDASH ...

As he does,

the smart-alecky young'uns—

no longer

acting ornery and brash—

bow their heads in shame

as if rightfully

taking the blame

FOR

the dastardly things

they had done-did

for eight months past.

BUT RED DWARF SMEGS . . .

One student,

Miss Maggie McPhee,

sitting amongst the renegades,

she, upon Mr. Boar's face,

HOLDS

her gaze steadfast.

WHY IS SHE DOING THIS?

Well, her brain,
much more than the others,
is busily absorbing
his <u>audacious</u> tongue-lash.

A-A-AH,

WOULD YOU BELIEVE?

As into her ears
flows Mr. Boar's <u>admonition</u>,
her mind is planning

a daring mission.

"Students," she hears,
"if you don't want to be poor
when you grow up,
then each of you had better
start filling up your learning cup;

BECAUSE

if you do not adopt

a firm determination
to obtain a good education,
be assured, poverty will likely become
your lifetime vocation."

OH,

BLINK, BLINK, BLINK,

AND

CA-POW, CA-WOW!

Mr. Boar's angry ranting
makes Miss Maggie McPhee

THINK, THINK, THINK,

LIKE

RIGHT NOW.

YES.

At that moment

fed up with her life's lot,

instantly her future

she starts to plot.

"HMM.

If I study hard and learn a lot,

MIGHT I

escape a lifetime of fraught?

YES! YES! YES!

I'm gonna do it.

And that means from this day forth,

I've got to give

book-learning an all-out shot."

AT HOME,

trapped in a petri dish
of abuse and economic deprivation—
her father's wages reflecting his

second-grade education—

Miss Maggie McPhee
is seldom
allowed to bath or
wash her hair

AND

is only allotted

the shabbiest
of clothes to wear.

AND

as the family's scapegoat,
she gets blamed
for everyone's woes.

OH, AND

in family matters
is she ever allowed a voice?

NO-O-O.

ALSO,

she has no choice

BUT

to endure her blended sibling's
finger-pointing, lame-blaming,

cop-out defaming,

along with kicks to her shins
and cuffs to her chin;

AND

to her despair,

the painful yanking

of her *more-often-than-not*

lice-infected hair.

OH, I DECLARE,

when forced to sit

upon a straight-back chair

AND

told to keep

her head hung low,

she,

with her hands

upon her knees,

makes less noise
than a swarm of fleas.

AND SCUTTLEBUTT TUSSLE . . .

As she sits submissively still
not moving a muscle—
or daring to express her will—

SHE,

in her mind <u>conjures</u> up scenes
of climbing and swinging
in sycamore trees,

AND OF

living long ago

in Native American teepees,

AND OF

crouching in a meadow,
hunting prey with a crossbow,

AND OF

chanting, *He loves me,*

he loves me not,

while plucking pedals off

an imaginary daisy.

ACTUALLY,

she fantasizes anything
just to keep from going crazy.

AND

Heavens to Murgatroyd,

when blamed
for mishaps the others have done—
knowing from her stepmother
she cannot run—

does she complain?

NO-o-o.

A-a-ah, from that,
she is smart enough to <u>refrain</u>.

AT SCHOOL,

Miss Maggie McPhee —
feeling ashamed and disgraced,

wearing the mask

of poverty's face —
endures the constant

shunning of classmates

who *never, ever* had to sing

the *Stuck-In-Poverty Blues.*

OF COURSE,

her snooty classmates —
they in hardship never <u>overwrought</u> —

_ar^e ^mo^re _in_to s^huⁿⁿiⁿg

thaⁿ ^car_in_g a^bou^t

her _sa_d lo_t.

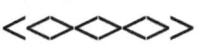

OH, LIP-SLICKER SLEWS . . .

Day in and day out,

her classmates ignore

the many clues

of her closeted abuse

even though

she sings naught

BUT

The Rags on My Back Blues.

YES,

her classmates are unaware

of the abuse,

she is forced to endure

under her stepmother's hateful glare.

WHY?

Because they know not
that besides going to bed ill-fed,
her psyche
—since a toddler—
has been growing numb,
tolerating the *bam, bam* firing gun
of her stepmother's

put-down spews.

BLIMEY,

her classmates have not a clue
that she must follow
her stepmother's

restrictive rule,

WHICH IS:

*Miss Maggie McPhee,
other than going to school,
you are never to venture past
the front yard gate.*

OH,

how does a youngster
endure such hate?

SUGAR-PUFF FLEAS . . .

Denied most *kid* opportunities,

she has no choice

but to endure and bemoan a fate

TO WHICH

her classmates cannot relate.

FOR CERTAIN,

they know not of her <u>dire plight</u>

because her lips,

under a fear-induced spell,
dare not to anyone tell
the haunt of her abusive hell.

OF COURSE,

she longs to escape

this horrid childhood fate,

but fear keeps her

from sharing a clue

about the hair-raising anguish

her stepmother is

putting her through.

DONKEY-HONK JAWS...

Although trapped

in her stepmother's abusive claws

with nary

a way to escape,

she, in her mind,
comes up with a plan
that will later *untwist* her fate.

"YES,"

thinks Miss Maggie McPhee,
"my stepmother can be

cruel and mean,

BUT

she cannot stop me
from fulfilling
my *educational* dream.

FOR PIG LATIN SWINE,

she has no idea

that in time,

I'll be fine

because I plan

to keep my nose to the grind.

AND TWIT, TWIT,

before she knows it,

I will *learn* my way through both

her abusive grapevine

AND

poverty's twisted twine."

<<><><>>

IN MAY OF 1953,

NONE OF

Miss Maggie McPhee's classmates,

LIKE SHE,

defined Mr. Boar's stern <u>exhortation</u> as a stunning revelation.

HOWEVER,

despite what her classmates did not know, she knew growing up she could not slow.

HONEYSUCKLE LATTICE . . .

Upon reaching adult status,

if poverty were to *smile up*

from her teacup,

she would surely

be the maddest.

UNLIKE CUD-CHEWING COWS . . .

Shortly after Mr. Boar's angry exhortation,

Miss Maggie McPhee

makes *nine* NO-WAY vows:

(ONE) ...

"NO WAY when I grow up,

do I want to be

stuck in poverty's rut,

<u>relegated</u>

to the *<u>wrong side of the tracks</u>*,

residing in a rundown,

<u>tar-papered</u> shack,

with nothing but

my hyper-alertness

guarding my aching,

overworked back."

(TWO) . . .

"NO WAY do I want

to turn into a mean,

p^eⁿⁿy-_pin_ch^{ing} g^{oa}t,

selling discarded <u>soda-pop bottles</u>—

each for a nickel—

just to stay afloat."[1]

(THREE) . . .

"NO WAY do I want

to cope forevermore

---

[1] When unemployed in the 1950s, her father did this to put bread on the table.

with landlords and bill collectors appearing

out of the blue,

pounding their fists upon my door
while boldly calling out,

'HEY, LADY,

your bill is way past due.
You had better pay up, or I will sue.'"

(FOUR) . . .

"NO WAY do I want to constantly sob

because I'm stuck

in a low-paying job

that offers

no chance to advance."

(FIVE) . . .

"NO WAY do I want

to be overburdened with strife,

chug, chugging

along on <u>two cylinders</u>

for the rest

of my life."

(SIX) . . .

"NO WAY do I want

to be bogged down

by dead-end reality,

mournfully singing

the latest *Blues*

while wishing my life

I could unconfuse."

(SEVEN) . . .

"NO WAY do I want

to end up dirt poor,

in emotional pain

with nothing to gain,

constantly reminding myself,

'HEY, GIRL,

your lack of education . . .
Well, you have only got

yourself to blame.'"

(EIGHT) . . .

"NO WAY do I want to look
into my children's eyes
while listening to
Mommy,
why can't we have it? cries."

(NINE) . . .

"NO WAY do I want
to face their youth and ashamedly

answer this truth:

'Listen, my dears,
our family has just a little bit
because sadly,
when younger, I quit.

FOR YOU SEE,

I failed to take

the education route;
I *failed* to get myself
turned about.'"

OH, MONKEY PUZZLE TREE . . .

As Miss Maggie McPhee

from poverty and abuse

hopes to get free,

she visualizes herself following
her educational plan

SO THAT HOPEFULLY,

when she grows up,
she will not have to endure

anything as bad as

her stepmother's hurtful swats

and nasty put-down potshots.

RICKETY
GARDEN GATES...

As Miss Maggie McPhee,

along with her classmates,

listens to Mr. Boar's spiel,

her receptive mind reels

with every word

he has to say,

ESPECIALLY:

"If you do not adopt
a firm determination
to obtain
a good education,

you could end up

with poverty being
your lifelong vocation."

THERE AIN'T GONNA BE ANY
LAZY SODA SIPPIN' SOW

because Mr. Boar's proclamation
prompts Miss Maggie McPhee

to make just ONE

YES-WAY VOW.

"YES WAY, I will study hard,

enhance my mind;

AND THEN,

when I grow up,
hopefully, I'll avoid poverty's bind."

BUT, RED ANT CULT . . .

Later, as a young adult,

sitting on the edge

of poverty's ledge,

COPING,

but not facing her woes . . .

WELL,

this is how her story goes.

SHE,

a frustrated kid,

desperately hoping
to rise above poverty
and the effects of abuse,

and yearning to become more
than her stepmother's label of

dimwitted goose,

AND

wanting to counter
society's put-down slams,

SUCH AS,

White trash girl,

get away from me.
Can't you see?

I won't be seen

with the likes of thee."

WELL,

GREEN RIVER BASS . . .

Miss Maggie McPhee,
staying <u>steadfast</u>
as a farmer's old ox,
longing for the chance to escape

poverty's box,

listens to every word
Mr. Boar has to say.

YES.

During

his tongue-lashing exhortation,

she hears him

spelling out

a poverty escape route

to which she, without doubt,

decides to steer.

TODAY,

one might ask,

"How can any youngster

possibly make any

educational gains

while being bombarded
by nasty putdown refrains

UNDER

the constant constraint
of a cruel stepmother's

oppressive thumb?"

TO BE HONEST,

Miss Maggie McPhee
did not stop to think about
how her future aspirations could thrive,

or even survive,

under her stepmother's

nasty imputations

and constant

PUT DOWN

degradations.

ZIPPING SAND FLEE . . .

Rather

than dwelling on her sad plight,

Miss Maggie McPhee—

keeping future <u>aspirations</u>
within her sight—

dares to hope

and dares to dream.

But most importantly,

she dares to believe

her firm determination
to obtain a *good* education
will give her the strength

to cope and scheme

until across poverty's threshold

she can slip

far beyond her stepmother's

abusive grip.

SWISHING HORSETAIL BRAIDS . . .

The summer between

sixth and seventh grade—

being treated worse than a criminal

under house arrest—

Miss Maggie McPhee,

with only her intelligence

keeping her from insanity's crest,

wHILES AWAY,

her summer vacation time

sitting infinitely still

upon her sentencing chair,
under her stepmother's
scowling stare.

THEN,

sully-eyed crow,

One hot, muggy day,

with her will to live

at an all-time low,

and she, in dire need of

a boost to her ego—

WHY,

what should pop into her mind

but a stunning revelation,

which instantly puts the squash

on her despair and frustration.

SWEET HONEYDEW VINES . . .

From out of the blue,

these amazing lines

prance, prance, prance

into her mind:

MISS MAGGIE MCPHEE,

no matter how much
poverty and abuse
have you in their bind,

remember,

only you

have total control

of your mind.

OH,

how her heart flutters
as she happily mutters
the best revelation she has had
in her *abusive* lifetime.

"MY MIND, MY MIND,

my mind is totally

MINE.

OH, YES,

she can hit me.

AND, YES,

she can spit on me.

AND, YES,

she can force me

to sit perfectly *still*

upon a straight-back chair.

AND, YES,

she can kick me in the shins.

AND, YES,

she can

deny me permission

to wash my hair.

BUT, NO,

she *cannot* control my *mind*

BECAUSE

my mind is totally

MINE."

HOT CRUMPETS AND TEA . . .

With her spirit uplifted,
Miss Maggie McPhee,
basking in

a glimmer of hope,

immediately starts focusing
on her educational scope.

OH, ANGELIC ELATION . . .

Bolstered by

her heaven-sent revelation,

she vows to stay on

the higher-educational route,

believing by studying hard,

she will escape

her stepmother's abusive clout.

AND

ALONG THE WAY,

she intends to slash her sash

to that

much-hated, put-down bash

OF

poor white trash.

As if invited to a stunning
Mother Hubbard "graded"

F - D - C - B - A

STAIRCASE BALL,

the next fall

with homework piled
three to five textbooks high,
Miss Maggie McPhee

Pushes her learning

way beyond the *D-D-D*
*D*ip and *D*iving seaweed

OF

near *F-F-F F*ailing.

THEN,

with nary a sign of trailing,
she sails through

the *C-C-C C*hoppy sea

of mediocrity

BEFORE

crossing over the *B-B-B B*ridge

of steady progress.

SOON

AFTERWARD,

aiming her learning arrow toward

the *A-A-A A*tmosphere

of *All-knowing,*

EXCELLENCE

becomes her Ally.

AND WOW.

As she accomplishes what
nobody expected her to do,
her spirit, like a hot-air balloon,
rides the air currents high in the sky.

NOW, IF TRUTH BE KNOWN,

everyone was <u>baffled</u>,
even Mr. Boar,
as to what caused
Miss Maggie McPhee's grades

to suddenly soar.

Sticks and stones
and flickering wicks,

YES,

to everyone's surprise,

one run-of-the-mill student
rises above her abusive mix
with an educational plan
she intends to make stick.

RAZZLE-DAZZLE BANSHEE . . .

Somehow, it escaped

everyone's attention
that Miss Maggie McPhee

had taken to heart

the warning that Mr. Boar
had felt compelled to impart.

YES. RIGHT UNDER

everyone's noses

on that long-ago day,
one poverty-stricken girl

secretly tucked away

every word Mr. Boar had to say
about the stupidity of twenty-nine
FAIRLY FINE cocky chicks
devoting *all* their study time

to rambunctious play.

OH,

WICKED WITCH DETHRONED . . .

Who could have predicted
in her seventh-grade year —

WITH

no special assistance
or backward-get-starters —
Miss Maggie McPhee

would play catch-up,

and stay up

despite taunts

from hate-brewing waters.

S-S-SH. DON'T TELL.

For you see,

she, a twelve-year-old,

fearing repercussions

if it were to be told,

decides to keep quiet

about her new learning ambition—

an ambition fueling

her efforts to undermine
her stepmother's
and poverty's coalition.

BUT

CRYING SHEEP BLEEPS...

wouldn't you know it?

Every six weeks
her report card betrays her

by boasting in *ink*

her *new learning conviction.*

SAD TO SAY,

her high marks

garner no honors or ribbons
or band-strutting stuff,

ONLY

a cruel stepmother yelling,
"BOHUNK, I've had
just about enough of your

show-off-ee stuff."

AT SCHOOL,

classmates taunting her

with

We're-better-than-thou claims —

WELL,

all their claims amount

to nothing more

THAN

downsized echoes

of Society's

<u>white trash</u> <u>disdains</u>.

AT HOME,

from cruel stepmother
come smarting smacks
across her face—

WHAM, BAM, SLAM—

AND

more than one nasty epigram.

"Bohunk,

just

who do you think

you are these days,

showing off with As?"

AT TIMES,

into the midst

of the family's

tar-paper shack squalor,

WHILE

her blended siblings stare

at the 21-inch TV

in their so-called parlor,

Miss Maggie McPhee,

sits at the kitchen table

doing homework,

ENDURING

ruler whacks across her knuckles

for *supposedly*

writing lessons *too* neat,

PLUS,

hate glares and shouts of,

"How dare you, you sneak?"

How dare she?

CLICKETY-CLACK CLOUT . . .

She dares because

she knows without a doubt

if she doesn't trudge forward,

she will suffer defeat.

OH, WARTHOG BROTHERS . . .

Despite her stepmother's
abusive stranglehold,
and having her feet stuck

in poverty's mold,

Miss Maggie McPhee
somehow manages to buck
Society's <u>condescending</u> stream

WHILE

holding fast

to her higher education dream.

BUT SULLY-BERRY TWIX...

For Miss Maggie McPhee
to rise above
her abusive mix,
she needs an escape plan
that will stick.

HEART-BEATING DRUMS...

At age fourteen comes
a change in the wind.

Running from
her stepbrother's molesting hands,
into a distant relative's home
Miss Maggie McPhee safely lands.

Loved and accepted,
she quickly snuggles in.

HALLELUJAH!

NO MORE

stepmother din.

No more sitting hours on a chair.
No more hearing:
"No. You cannot wash your hair."

AND TALK ABOUT

A SNICKERDOODLE DREAM . . .

Mm. Yum, yum.

In her

new home's garage freezer,

she stumbles across

five gallons

of chocolate ice cream.

SAD SEXIST MANIFEST . . .

Who could have guessed?

THAT

Three months later

on her new home's *nicety* stage,

Miss Maggie McPhee's educational dream

would get beaten down

by an unfair

sex discrimination a̲d̲a̲g̲e̲?

THAT BEING:

A GIRL

DOESN'T NEED

TO GO TO COLLEGE?

"Unattainable, unreachable,"

her elders decisively say,

as they negate

her dream to attend college one day.

"But...but...but..."

her lips do plead.

"NO BUTS...

Listen, young lady,

A GIRL

DOESN'T NEED

TO GO TO COLLEGE,"

her mind, they constantly feed.

OH,

YUCKY HORSE-PUCKY HAY . . .

Her elders' <u>resolute adage</u>,
for certain, darkens her day.

"College prep,"

her lips do voice,

"is my *first* educational choice.

Please, please, please?"

"NO, NO, NO."

Her elders'

thumbs-down answers,

riv-riv-riveting

her mind . . .

WELL, WHEW!

They feel like
the drilling stingers
of a *thousand* maverick bees.

"No. You cannot.

No. You will not,"
her mind, they constantly feed.

Oh, how she hates

their *no-college* creed.

TO HER MISFORTUNE,

it matters not

how much she pleads.
Her elders' declaration,

"A GIRL

DOESN'T NEED

TO GO TO COLLEGE,"

makes clear . . . her river of tears,
they will NOT heed.

<<><><>>

"But…but…but…"

"Listen, young Lady.

Setting your sights
on an impossible dream
will do nothing
but make you sadder."

"But…but…but…"

"Listen, young Lady.

There's *no possible way* for you
to climb the higher education ladder."

"But…but…but…"

"Listen, young Lady.

After high school,
you will need to make a living."

"But…but…but…"

"Listen, young Lady.

IT IS FINAL.

Permission for college prep
we are not giving."

WRETCHED SWAMP FLEAS...

From Miss Maggie McPhee's
quivering lips, her

but, but, buts fade

as she walks away
with her head hung low
as if waylaid by Deadly Nightshade.

SADLY,

after her elders
make this crystal clear:

"ONTO

the Higher Education Avenue
we will NOT sign permission

for you to steer,"
Miss Maggie McPhee

accepts as truth,

their resolute adage, i.e.,

A GIRL

DOESN'T NEED

TO GO TO COLLEGE.

At this point,
realizing her destiny
lies within their power,

SHE,

under their intimidation,

does <u>naught</u> but <u>cower</u>.

FOR SHE KNOWS

only they, *as her guardians,*

have the right to sign

her educational destiny
on the school forms dotted line.

TO HER,

it doesn't seem fair;

BUT

it makes no difference
what she doth voice,

she can do naught

BUT

accept

their educational choice.

LATER,

choking back remorse,

she watches them

checking the box

next to: Commercial Course

AND THEN

jotting their names below hers
on the school form's
parental-approval line.

Ah, knowing

she is not

going to get her way,
she halfheartedly
succumbs to the doom

of being misled

by what her *caring*,
yet *unwise* elders said,

I.E.,

"A GIRL DOESN'T NEED TO GO TO COLLEGE."

OH, CRISS-CROSS ARMORY...

With her heart and mind

now locked in a

p_us^h-p^ul^l <u>q</u>uaⁿd^{ary,}

Miss Maggie McPhee

feels nothing but dismay.

THUS,

WITH THEIR WORDS:

Do as we say,
and you will thank us someday,
constantly ringing in her ears,

AND, ALSO,

shortly after signing,
knowing signatures are binding,

she starts pining.

"OH,

why did I sign on that line?

Was I afraid to go

against their will?

AFRAID? YES, BUT

ANGRY is the better word.

DAGNABBIT!

Angry I am still

because on that day,
after hearing
my guardian mother say,
"Dear, just sign on that line

and you will see

everything

will turn out fine,"

STUPID ME,

I, like a programmed robot,

picked up that pen

AND

scribbled my name

on the student-designated line."

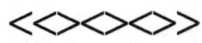

NOT SURPRISINGLY,

shortly after signing,
Miss Maggie McPhee
becomes

o v e r w h e l m e d

with anguish.

"GIRL,

whatever were you thinking?

WHY,

you signed that paper

without even blinking.

HEAVENS
TO MURGATROYD . . .

You <u>nixed</u> what you cherish.

Now, your dream

will surely perish."

IMMEDIATELY

following her heart's <u>lament</u>,

this advice her mind

does promptly counter-vent:

"HEY, GIRL,

STOP! STOP! STOP!

Stop tormenting your soul.
Fretting about

what can't be undone

is *not* worth the emotional toll.
Besides, you need to concede
that your elders know

what's best for you.

SO,

FOR PITY'S SAKE,

stop this *poor-me* nonsense.

Just accept that you did

what you were

supposed to do."

Half-heartedly convinced

her dream now lies

beyond her reach,

and having learned

it does no good

to cry and screech,

YET,

needing to find solitude—

to think,

to sort,

to figure out

what to conclude—

Miss Maggie McPhee

runs beyond the barnyard line,

straight through

a stand of tall white pine.

Down the hill

and through a ravine,

she runs until she comes

to a shallow stream.

THERE,

far away from curious eyes,
she, sitting upon a granite boulder,
sinks into a solitude that
only nature can <u>exude</u>.

As fresh tears mesh

with her emotional pain,
she sobbingly says,

"Why do I whine?

What right

do I have to complain?

My guardians are so kind.

And I'm just a kid.

OH,

PLEASE TELL ME,

my aching heart,

why do you NOT convey

that my elders are right

in what they say?

YES, I KNOW.

I have all the food I want to eat—"

"AND,"

intrudes *her mental wit*,

"I do believe, Miss Maggie McPhee,

that neither one

upon

your back doth beat.

AND SAY,

every night,

don't you lay down your head

upon a comfy bed?"

"WHY, YES, I DO, BUT—"

"And don't your elders provide you

with nice clothes to wear?"

"OF COURSE, THEY DO."

"And unlike your stepmother,
who treated you so unfair,

does either one say,

'Miss Maggie McPhee,
this week you cannot
wash your hair?'"

"WELL, NO, BUT—"

"Crimp-tailed catfish, Miss,
do you want to lose all this?"

"U-U-UH, UH, NO. I DON'T."

"Then yin-yang swirl,

listen up, girl.

TO STOP

this binge of malcontent,

ignore the pull

of your heart's lament.
Truly accept
your elders' adage,

THAT

A GIRL

DOESN'T NEED

TO GO TO COLLEGE."

Half-heartedly believing

she has

nothing to gain

BY

bucking her elders'

A GIRL

DOESN'T NEED

TO GO TO COLLEGE

REFRAIN,

Miss Maggie McPhee, forcing a smile,

puts the *kibosh*

on her emotional pain.

THEN,

HOT BISCUIT BITS . . .

She,

no longer consumed

w i t h   t i z z y   f i t s,

visualizes herself

burying her college dream

beneath the granite rock

upon which she dauntingly sits.

THEN, LIKE A SQUASHED PIE,

believing her dream

will lie

buried "forevermore"

beneath that stone's hard rock core,

AND

assuming no one
will *ever* listen
to what she wants to voice,

she walks away

convinced she did right
by accepting her elder's
educational choice.

BRAINWASHED DOOMED

BUT

no longer consumed

with frustration and wrath,
she retraces her steps
back along nature's path.

AS SHE DOES,

all in her mind

that seems to <u>tarry</u>
are her guardians' words,

You need to take

the <u>Commercial Course</u>;
you need to become a secretary.

SADLY,

all through her formative years,

they constantly say,

You need, you need;
and she, forever hearing,
You need, you need —

WELL,

these words in her thoughts,
she dutifully *<u>kneads</u>* and *<u>heeds</u>*.

REGRETTABLY,

these acts, over time,

cement in her mind

(AS TRUTH)

her elders' dis-knowledge that

A GIRL

DOESN'T NEED

TO GO TO COLLEGE.

SCUDDLE-BUTT PEEVE...

At age eighteen,
young and naïve
Miss Maggie McPhee,

believing marriage

will be the answer

to *all* her hopes and prayers,

foolishly expects

her "I do" leap

to protect her

from all of life's hellish <u>snares</u>.

BUT THE TRUTH SOON FLOWS.

Neither her mate nor she knows

what true love

is or

should be.

SAD TO SAY,

that fact,

clashing with reality,

causes another

marriage fatality.

ROBIN EGG BLUE,

two years

after saying *I do,*

the county judge <u>sanctions</u>

the couple's divorce decree,

awarding custody

of their infant son

to Miss Maggie McPhee.

Clutching
a <u>stenographer</u>'s tablet
in her hand,

A SECRETARIAL JOB

Miss Maggie McPhee
shortly does land.

AH, BUT . . .

believing she has

no bargaining power,

she immediately accepts

the company's first offer

of a dollar eighty-nine an hour.

HIGH DIDDLE DEE DUM . . .

In the years to come,

she pays rent and daycare,

utilities and bus fare,

and wears her clothes until threadbare.

YES,

like a steadfast fool,

she does naught
but what in high school
she had been taught.

THUS,

believing typing, filing, and
transcribing shorthand
will for life be her lot,

she becomes adept

at functioning like
a programmed robot.

"Hey, Miss Maggie McPhee."

"YEAH, UH . . .

Are you talking to me?"

"YES, I AM."

"Who are you?

And
what do you want?"

"I'm your subconscious.

AND, MY DEAR,

what I want is to remind you
that a *Strong Interest Test*
in high school years ago
showed a career in social services
as the direction

for you to go."

"YES, I KNOW.

But don't you see?

I didn't get a college degree."

"HOLY TOLEDO, GIRL.

Twelve years have rolled by
in the blink of an eye."

"YEAH.

And it would be a lie

if I were to deny

THAT

my heart has constantly bled
from accepting what my *caring*
yet unwise elders
drummed into my head."

"O-O-OH.

And what might that be?"

"Come on. You know. It's

A GIRL

DOESN'T NEED

TO GO TO COLLEGE."

NOW, THIS ADAGE,

which Miss Maggie McPhee's elders had long ago sung,

draws her back

to when
she was young,
to when the tearful words,

but, but, but . . .

more than once

rolled off her tongue.

THIEVIN' BLUE JAYS . . .

As she recalls
her youthful days,
a voice from the past

comes barreling in,

making her feel guilty of sin.

"HEY, GIRL,

you agreed to do

as your elders said.

REMEMBER?"

"Of course, I remember."

"Then, hear me out.

LOOK, GIRL.

It's high time you stopped

this *but, but, but* crud,

and let your elders' adage,

A GIRL

DOESN'T NEED

TO GO TO COLLEGE,

flow freely through your blood.

AND DON'T FORGET.

You *need,* **you** *need,* you *need*

to keep k̲n̲e̲ading

your elders' *needed* m̲a̲n̲n̲a̲ bread."

"NO-O-O,

NO, NO-O-O.

It's too much of a chore.

BESIDES,

kneading my elders'

needed m̲a̲n̲n̲a̲ bread,

doesn't

sit right with me anymore."

NOT LONG

after that revelation,

Miss Maggie McPhee,

peering through a foggy mist,

witnesses a swarm of protestors

on the march,

demanding liberation.

OH

HORSEFLY REDEMPTION . . .

Upon closer inspection,

she spots no men,

nor nary a munchkin.

ONLY A THRONG OF WOMEN,

with their feet

firmly anchored

in a sea of resolute gumption.

FORTUNATELY,

her eyes,

her mind—

and her heart, too—

are receptive to seeing

THAT,

women of all colors and creeds—

bearing no shame,

their hearts aflame—
are finding the courage
to collectively proclaim:

"WE, AS WOMEN,

for too many generations,
have been economically slighted,
educationally blighted,

AND,

for too long, considered

subservient to men."

As she listens to this <u>ideology</u>, Miss Maggie McPhee realizes these brave soldiers

OF

<u>The Women's Liberation Movement</u>—

armed *only* with the

power of the pen—

are heightening Society's awareness

ABOUT

the unfairness

of *women* being treated

as <u>subservient</u> to *men*.

FROM AFAR,

she watches as they

brazenly march forth,

shouting equality <u>convictions,</u>

and demanding

an end to

<u>*differential*</u> pay <u>subscriptions</u>.

IN DUE TIME,

into the minds of their sisters

(including Miss Maggie McPhee's),

women of this Movement

boldly, bravely sow

their equality <u>convictions</u>

WHILE

tactfully countering

their sisters' misters' grumblings

AND

high-hat conniptions.

ACROSS AMERICA

female voices proclaim:

WE, AS WOMEN,

*demand the right
to make our own choices.*

BUSINESS WORLD,

WE, AS WOMEN,

*expect our due.
Lesser pay than men,
we will no longer
accept from you.*

AND,

WE, AS WOMEN,

will not bend.

We deserve,

we want,

We demand

<u>equivalent</u> pay for doing

the same work as men.

GRADUALLY,

with this sisterhood,

Miss Maggie McPhee

finds herself linking.

THEN,

as this group's edicts realign

her faulty thinking,

she grips her past's disarray,

AND

with one mighty fling,
she throws it far, far away.

SOON AFTERWARD,

Miss Maggie McPhee
is bombarded by opposing forces
coming at her
from two different <u>concourses</u>.

THE FIRST,

she stubbornly fights.

THE SECOND,

she claims as her right.

CA-POW. CA-POW.

Turning toward the first,
she hears,

"Young lady,
come along now.

You need, you need —

LISTEN.

You *need* to keep eating
your elders' manna bread."

"But, but, but . . ."

"Young lady, LOOK.
Your bowl is full.

SO,

do not tarry.

You *need* to carry on

as a *secretary*."

"U-U-UH,

you don't understand.
See, I, Miss Maggie McPhee,

hate that

you-need manna bread.

AND

down that confining path
I no longer want to <u>tread</u>."

FROSTED FIDDLEHEAD FERNS

As Miss Maggie McPhee turns

in the opposite direction,

she hears the *other voice*

t r u m p e t i n g   f o r t h

a *different* choice.

"Okay, sister. Listen up.

It is not too late

to change your fate."

"REALLy?"

"YEs.

come along now.

It's time you find the courage
to get rid of the baggage
of your elders' adage."

"REALLy?

But, but, but,

how do I do that?"

"JUMPIN' JIMINY CRICKET, GIRL,

ALL

you have to do is

say, 'POOH to A GIRL DOESN'T NEED TO GO TO COLLEGE.'"

"POOH? THAT'S ALL?"

"YES. JUST SAY POOH."

"WHAT?

You're expecting me

to get rid of the baggage
of my elders' <u>adage</u>
by just saying

POOH

TO

A GIRL

DOESN'T NEED

TO GO TO COLLEGE?"

"Yes, my dear, that,

PLUS,

you must voice

a *new* conviction,

one of your *own* volition."

"You mean something like this:

'To my elders,

I will no longer cower.

INSTEAD,

I will strip away

the illogical power

that for years has professed

their *dis*-knowledge, i.e., that

A GIRL DOESN'T NEED TO GO TO COLLEGE.'

AND

to accomplish this,

I will visualize myself
standing
at the edge
of a deep canyon ledge,
flinging their subservient verbiage
to the rocks below.

AND AS I DO,

I will scream,

Death to such <u>dis-knowledge</u>.

AND

SNICKERDOODLE FRITZ . . .

Afterward,

I will shout this:

'It's *not* that this girl *needs*,

BUT RATHER,

she *wants* to go to college.'

SO,

pOOH, pOOH, pOOH,

to my elder's adage.

Oh, POOH to

A GIRL

DOESN'T NEED

TO GO TO COLLEGE.

There. I said it.

I mean it.

And to it, I vow

to no longer kowtow."

After voicing her new conviction,

nothing stops Miss Maggie McPhee.

Truly relieved of the baggage
of her elders' old adage,

she shouts with glee,

"Being a woman,

I can do anything.

YES.

It matters not
what anyone else voices,

I have the right

to make my own choices."

THEN,

visualizing herself journeying
through brush, briar
and scary swampy mire,

SHE,

in her mind,

slipping back in time,

eagerly takes stock
of a familiar granite rock.

OH,

FLIP-FLAP THUNDER . . .

Like a pirate about to <u>plunder</u>,

she drops to one knee,

kisses the granite marker—

<u>stalwart</u>,

yet weathered darker—

knowing full well

THAT

her higher-education dream

lies buried beneath it,

waiting for her

to set it free.

AS GEESE DO FLOCK,

she digs beneath that rock,
through sands of time,
while saying,

"It's about time

I reclaim what is rightfully mine."

WILD HORSE TAMING . . .

Believe it or not,
at the same time, she hears
an <u>ethereal</u> voice proclaiming,

Dreams, my dear,

never die.
They merely wait

for their bearers to realize that

it is never too late

to take charge

of one's fate.

As Miss Maggie McPhee

gives her dream full reign,

it, wasting no time,

catapults her

eager-to-learn mind

onto the college scene.

AFTER SETTING HER LEARNING GOALS,

Miss Maggie McPhee,
for eight arduous years,
juggles
parental and student roles

while tapping the sap

of the higher education tree

until fully winged

WITH

her master's degree.

FINALLY,

her dream is fulfilled. She graduates.

DESERVEDLY,

she takes a little time to celebrate.
Then, seeking a new career to ply,

she spreads her wings and

soars Eagle High.

AH, YES.

Setting her sights

on more than sheep-giblet pie,

she,

without hesitation,

flies straight away

into opportunity's

wide-open sky.

TODAY,

enjoying retirement,
Miss Maggie McPhee
looks back at her

SOCIAL SERVICE CAREER

AND

willingly professes,

"The seeds to my success
came neither from demanding
a handout while crying,

Foul play,

nor from pitifully begging,

Please. Ple-e-ease,

do it for me,

for can't you see,

poverty's claws

are clutching me like prey.

QUITE THE CONTRARY,

when I,

as a young girl,

decided to break poverty's yoke

and to also cut my sash

from the derogatory label

of poor white trash . . .

WELL,

BLOOMIN' FINESSE,

back in 1953,
I doubt anyone would have guessed
that happiness and success—
life's pinnacles of paradise—
would unfurl for me,

a poor, abused girl,

by adhering to
Mr. Boar's advice,

I.E.,

You can dispel forevermore
poverty from clawing
at your life's door,

ᶦf you are willing

to meet the challenge
of education's hard-learning chore."

TODAY,
ENJOYING THE FRUITS

of her determination,
Miss Maggie McPhee,

elatedly, and belatedly,

humbly says,
"Thank you, Mr. Boar
(in real life, Mr. Moore),
for challenging me to change my diet

of ignorant manna

at Pine Township Elementary School
in Michigan City, Indiana.

INDEED,

I will always remember

the shame I endured

on that fateful day in May of 1953

when you pitted me

AND

my classmates against

your fifth-grade students in your

Let-us-see-

who-has-learned-

better-this-year

SPELLING BEE."

Young minds, after

digesting this saga,

Miss Maggie McPhee
hopes you will take heed
of Mr. Boar's creed,

I.E.,

Adopting a firm determination
to obtain a good education
is, quite frankly, the best way

to keep poverty at bay.

LASTLY,

as she says farewell,
Miss Maggie McPhee (i.e., me, the author)
leaves you
with these words of wisdom:

Nothing can destroy you
if you view everything
coming your way in life—
both the good
and the bad—
as a gift.

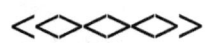

GLOSSARY

GLOSSARY
(Includes Author's Notes)

abide (verb) – to accept without opposition or question; to endure, tolerate, withstand.

abound, abounded (verb) – to occur or exist in great quantities, plentiful.

absurd (adjective) – meaningless, silly.

abyss (noun) – deep hole.

accentuate, accentuated (verb) – to give emphasis.

adage (noun) – a traditional saying expressing a common experience or observation.

adamant (adjective) – unyielding, stubborn, unbending.

adept (adjective) – skilled, expert, clever.

admonition (noun) – warning, scolding.

allotted (verb) – given.

anguish (noun) – distress, suffering.

arduous (adjective) – difficult, involving great hardship or exertion, laborious.

arrogance (noun), arrogant (adjective) – a feeling of superiority, overbearing conduct, conceit, self-importance.

aspiration, aspirations (noun) – strong desire, ambition, longing, or aim.

audacity (noun), audacious (adjective) – boldness or daring, with confidence or arrogance.

band-strutting (adjective) – AUTHOR'S NOTE: In this story, it implies happily tooting praises for a job well done.

banshee (noun) – ghost, spirit.

basking (verb) – enjoying, delighting in.

bellowing (verb) – shouting, roaring, yelling, hollering.

besieged (verb) – overwhelmed.

blight, blighted (verb) – any cause of impairment, destruction, or ruin.

bohunk (noun) – a put-down, disparaging term used to discriminate against unskilled foreign-born laborers, especially those immigrating to the United States from east-central or southeastern Europe. AUTHOR'S NOTE: It was common in the late 1800s/early 1900s for more settled people to *look down on* and taunt newer immigrants. Most likely, Maggie's stepmother learned the term, bohunk, from her parents and/or grandparents. Thus, since her stepmothers' *English* family had been in this country much longer than her birth mother's *Slovakian* family, they may have felt superior.

bombard, bombarded (verb) – to attack, to direct loud angry words toward someone.

brash (adjective) – pushy, loud, foolhardy.

briar (noun) – a tangled mess of prickly plants.

brow (noun) – ridge over the eye.

capacity (noun) – the actual or potential ability to do something, the power of receiving impressions and knowledge.

captivate, captivated (verb) – to enthrall, to charm.

castrate, castrated (verb) – deleting certain things, purging.

catapult, catapults (verb) – launch, hurl, propel.

coalition (noun) – an alliance, especially a temporary one between persons; a partnership.

commercial course – AUTHOR'S NOTE: In the 1950s, an educational tract (including typing, shorthand, bookkeeping, and business law) offered to high school students who wanted to become secretaries.

compel, compelled (verb) – to have a powerful and irresistible effect.

complicity (noun) – support, participation.

concede (verb) – acknowledge, admit, accept, own.

concourse, concourses (noun) – A large open space for accommodating crowds.

condescend, condescending (adjective) – behaving as if one is conscious of descending from a superior position.

conjures (verb) – summons, calls up.

conniptions (noun) – fits of anger, hysteria, or the like.

conniving (adjective) – scheming, devious.

constraint (noun) – control, restriction.

construe (verb) – understand, see.

conviction, convictions (noun) – a fixed belief.

copious (adjective) – plentiful, bountiful.

country hick – SEE hick below.

cowardice (noun) – lack of courage to face danger, difficulty, or opposition.

cuffs (noun) – a hit with the hand.

dauntingly (adverb) – dismayingly.

defaming (verb) – offending, vilifying.

degradations (noun) – the act of degrading or humiliating.

degrade (verb) – to lower in dignity, bring into contempt, to lower in character or quality.

deprivation (noun) – poverty, scarcity

derogatory (adjective) – insulting, offensive, belittling. AUTHOR'S NOTE: Wrongfully saying something negative about someone, putting a person down.

designated (adjective) – defined.

despondent (adjective) – glum, unhappy, miserable, sad, discouraged.

dictate, dictated (verb) – to command with authority, to give orders, an authoritative order or command.

dictate, dictated (verb) – to say or read aloud something for another to write down. AUTHOR'S NOTE: Before the widespread use of computers, employers dictated letters to secretaries who wrote down what they said verbatim in shorthand in stenographer tablets, then, they transcribed the shorthand into either letters or business forms on a typewriter.

differential (adjective) – differences or diversity AUTHOR'S NOTE: In this story, it refers to women being paid far less than men for the same type of work.

dim-witted (adjective) – slang or put-down term referring to a slow-thinking person.

dire (adjective) – awful, terrible, horrible.

disarray (noun) – confusion, disorder.

disdain, disdains (noun) – to look upon or treat with contempt, despise, scorn.

dis-knowledge (noun) – something that isn't true that one chooses to believe as truth.

dispel (verb) – to drive off, scatter, disperse something.

doth (verb) – an archaic (antiquated, old) form of the words do and does.

edict, edicts (noun) – decree, authoritative command.

equivalent (adjective) – equal in value, measure, force, or significance.

ethereal (adjective) – heavenly or celestial, of the ether or upper regions of space.

exhortation (noun) – The conveyance of urgent advice.

exude (verb) – give out, release, radiate.

faltering (verb) – hesitating, showing uncertainty.

felicity (noun) – delight, joy, happiness.

fictive kin – AUTHOR'S NOTE: An African American term referring to people who are not blood-related but have an on-going, close-as-blood relationship.

figuratively (adverb) – not literal or direct, symbolically.

fraught (verb) – burdened, weighed down

fray (noun) – worn part with loose threads.

frayed (adjective) – i.e., frayed rope.

garner, garners, garnered (verb) – to gather in or collect, to get, acquire.

gender (noun) – Male or female sex category, characteristics, or role.

Gondwanaland (noun) – a hypothetical continent that (according to plate tectonic theory) broke up later into India, Australia, Africa, South America, and Antarctica.

grit, grits, gritting (verb) – grind the teeth.

grueling (adjective) – requiring great effort.

gumption (noun) – initiative, courage, spunk.

hawk (verb) – to call aloud.

hiatus (noun) – break, gap, space.

hick (noun) – an offensive term referring to a rural, unsophisticated person, often poorly educated.

hype, hypes (verb) – buildup, something overpublicized.

ideology (noun) -- beliefs

i.e. – that is to say, namely, specifically, to be exact.

illogical (adjective) – contrary to or disregarding the rules of logic, unreasoning.

immersed (verb) – plunged or sunk in, to involve deeply.

impart (verb) – to make known, tell, relate, to give.

implosion (noun) – crumbling, cave-in, disintegration.

imputation, imputations (noun) – fault-finding, accusation, insinuation.

infinitely (adjective) – extremely.

intimidate (verb), intimidation (noun) – to make timid; to inspire with fear; to overawe with a forceful personality or superior display of fame, power, or wealth.

juts (verb) – extending beyond the main body or line.

kibosh (noun) – stoppage, halt, or prevention of something from happening.

knead, kneading (verb) – work, mold.

kowtow, kowtowing (verb) – to act in an excessively subservient manner.

lament, laments (noun, verb) – cry, wail.

languish – to pine with desire or longing, melancholy.

levitate (verb) – to cause to rise or float in the air.

lot (noun) – allotted share or portion, a distinct portion, or partial portion of anything.

manna (noun) – divine or spiritual food. AUTHOR'S NOTE: In this story, manna bread refers to the ideals that the elders "fed" the girl's mind.

nary (adjective) – not any.

mediocrity (noun) – average, ordinary.

mesmerize, mesmerized (verb) – compel by fascination, in awe, absorb somebody's attention.

metaphor (noun) – a figure of speech in which a word or phrase that ordinarily means one thing is used of another thing to suggest a likeness between the two.

midst (noun) – the figurative area into which a group is gathered.

mire (noun), miring (verb) – to sink in the mire (swampy ground, bog, marsh) or mud; to cause to stick fast in the mire.

munchkin (noun) – a small child.

mundane (adjective) – ordinary, commonplace, unexciting.

naïve (adjective); naïvely (adverb) – having or showing a lack of experience, judgment or information.

naught (noun) – nothing, to regard or treat as no importance.

negate (verb) – disprove, deny.

nix, nixed (verb) – to stop.

odious (adjective) – horrible, revolting.

oppressive (adjective) – cruel, harsh, unjust.

overwrought (adjective) – stressed, distraught, fatigued.

parlor (noun) – a room for the reception and entertainment of visitors; a living room. AUTHOR'S NOTE: Before the 1960s, many families, no matter how rich or poor, referred to their living room as the parlor, especially on the East Coast.

parody (noun) – a humorous or satirical imitation of an event.

petri dish (noun) – a shallow, circular glass dish with a loose cover, used in the preparation of bacteriological cultures. In this story, it is used as a metaphor, which is a figure of speech in which a word or phrase that ordinarily means one thing is used of another thing to suggest a likeness between the two.

pining (verb) – yearning, longing, wishing, desiring.

plight (noun) – an unfavorable situation.

plunder (verb) – to rob of goods or valuables by open force.

potshots (noun) – unfounded criticism.

professed (adjective) – declare something falsely, declare something openly, express faith in a particular belief.

psyche(s) (noun) – the human soul, spirit, or mind.

punitive (adjective) – punishing.

quandary (noun) – dilemma, fix, predicament, catch-22.

quell (verb) – to suppress, put an end to, to subdue, quiet.

razor strap (noun) – AUTHOR'S NOTE: A long leather strap that men used to swish their long razor edges across to hone or clean before lathering up and shaving. In homes that had no bathrooms, shaving soap and a brush for lathering were usually stored in a mug by the kitchen sink and the razor strap was hung nearby.

realign, realigns (verb) – to again arrange in a straight line, to adjust again, to again bring into line.

refrain, refrains (noun) – a phrase or verse recurring at intervals, something repeated often.

reign (verb) – to have the supreme rule, power, or influence.

relegated (verb) – to send or consign to an inferior position, place, or condition.

remiss (adjective) negligent, lax, inattentive.

renegades (noun) – rebels.

repercussions (noun) – an action set in motion by an event or action, the result of an action, rebound, or consequence.

resignedly (adverb) – submissive, unresisting, give up.

resolute (adjective) – firmly resolved or determined.

rivet, riveting (verb) – to hold the interest or attention of a person; to fasten or fix firmly with a rivet, to hammer to secure something.

saga (noun) – a chronology or narrative of events or achievements.

sanctioned (verb) – to authorize, approve, or allow.

sash (noun) – a cord, ribbon or belt that is attached or bound to something.

scapegoat (noun) – culprit, fall guy/gal.

scope (noun) – possibility, choice.

shabbiest (adjective) – ragged, tattered.

shanty (noun) – a crudely built hut, cabin, or house.

shantytown (adjective/noun) – a community with crudely built huts, cabins or houses.

shirttail relatives – AUTHOR'S NOTE: A term used to describe relatives two or more generations removed.

shoe-station (adjective), shoe station (noun) – AUTHOR'S NOTE: A term created by Maggie's stepmother, i.e., *"Bohunk, keep those eyes on your shoe station . . ."* meaning: "Keep staring at your shoes."

shorthand (noun) – a method of rapid handwriting using simple strokes, abbreviations, or symbols that designate letters, words, or phrases. AUTHOR'S

NOTE: After businesses became dependent on computers, shorthand became obsolete and is no longer taught.

shunning (verb) – rejected, ignored, turned away from.

simulating (verb) – imitating, mimicking.

slothful (adjective) – sluggish, inactive.

snared, snares (verb) – entrap, entangle, or catch unawares.

soda pop bottles (noun) – AUTHOR'S NOTE: In the 1950s, before laws made littering a finable offense, poor people (and children needing pocket change) scrounged along ditches and highways for discarded soda pop bottles and redeemed them for five cents each at grocery stores or gas stations. The poor often used this money to purchase bread—about ten to fifteen cents a loaf in the 1950s.

spews (verb) – to cast forth, gush, or eject.

spouts, spouting (verb) – to state or declaim volubly (continuous flow of words) or in an oratorical (art of public speaking) manner.

squalor (noun) – wretchedness, dirtiness.

stalwart (adjective) – firm, steadfast, uncompromising.

steadfast (adjective) – firm, as in purpose; resolution; firmly fixed in place or position.

stenographer (noun) – a person skilled in writing shorthand symbols, usually in a stenographer's tablet.

subscriptions (noun) – a sum of money given or pledged as a contribution, investment, etc. AUTHOR'S NOTE: In this story, it refers to the sum of money an employer agrees to pay for work done.

subservient (adjective) – serving or acting in a subordinate capacity, of lesser importance, too eager to obey.

succumbs (verb) – to give way to superior force, yield.

tai chi (noun) (pronounced tie jee) – an ancient Chinese form of graceful exercise.

taint, tainted (verb) – infect, contaminate, corrupt, pollute, or spoil something.

tantalization (noun) – temptation.

tar paper (adjective) shanty (noun) – AUTHOR'S NOTE: Tarpaper is a heavy tarred paper used as a sublayer for siding or a roof. Years ago, the term tar paper shanty or shack was used to describe an old, dilapidated, unfinished or poorly constructed home. When the cost of siding was prohibitive, low-income people resorted to tacking tarpaper over shiplap (scrap lumber). Inside a tar paper shanty or shack, discarded newspapers stuffed or tacked between two-by-fours served as insulation. Unfortunately, this created a fire hazard. If there was no wallboard in the home, old sheets, old quilts, or yards of cheap material were hung in doorways to provide privacy. If there was no kitchen plumbing, a "slop" bucket was used to catch wastewater from the kitchen sink, which when full, was thrown out the back door. Either a well or an outside hand pump was the source of water. As late as the 1950s, some of these tar paper shacks still didn't have electricity or indoor plumbing.

tarry (verb) – to remain, linger, wait, to delay or be tardy in acting, loiter.

tenacity (noun), tenacious (adjective) – determined or stubborn, tightly held, persistent, not easily disconnected.

threshold (noun) – any place or point of entering or beginning.

throng (noun) – a multitude of people crowded or assembled.

transcribe, transcribing (verb) – to make a written or typewritten copy of dictated material.

transfixed (Verb) – rooted to the spot

tread (verb) – to step or walk on, about, in or along; to trample or crush underfoot.

trudge (verb) – to walk laboriously or wearily.

trumpeting (verb) – to proclaim loudly.

tumultuous (adjective) – noisy, rowdy, wild.

two cylinders (adjective) – AUTHOR'S NOTE: The saying, "She only operates on two cylinders" implies she is not working or cannot work up to normal capacity.

unattainable (adjective) – unable to reach, achieve, or accomplish; unable to obtain.

unheeded (verb) – to be inattentive, ignore.

verbiage (noun) – overabundance or superfluity of words.

vocation (noun) – career, job, occupation, work.

volition (noun) – choosing, ability to choose, desire.

waning (adjective – weakening, fading

waylaid (verb) – ambushed.

White trash (noun, adjective) – poor Whites collectively. AUTHOR'S NOTE: In the 1950s—with the class division based on economic status—if you were poor and White, you were considered *poor White trash* and made to feel of lesser value.

woeful (adjective) – unhappy, distressed.

Women's Liberation Movement – a movement to gain full educational, social, and economic opportunities for women equal to those which men are traditionally understood to have.

wretched (adjective) – unhappy, miserable.

wrong side of the tracks or other side of the tracks – AUTHOR'S NOTE: In the 1950s Railroad tracks were figuratively viewed as the dividing line between the "haves" and the "have-nots." The snubbing of the poor, actually anyone who tried to move upward was commonplace.

Commenting on the site where this parody was purchased will be very much appreciated by the author.

www.ingramcontent.com/pod-product-compliance
Lightning Source LLC
LaVergne TN
LVHW041541070426
835507LV00011B/859